The Ultimate Guide to Peanut Farming

A Practical Handbook for Raising and
Selling Peanuts

Introduction

Peanuts are not just a delicious snack, but an incredibly versatile crop with endless potential for profit and sustainability. However, mastering the art of peanut farming is no easy feat, and even seasoned farmers can face challenges in raising and selling these legumes. That's why we are thrilled to present "The Ultimate Guide to Peanut Farming: A Practical Handbook for Raising and Selling Peanuts." From choosing the perfect plot of land to navigating the complex world of peanut marketing, this comprehensive guide covers everything you need to know to achieve success in the peanut farming industry. With practical techniques, expert advice, and real-world examples, this guide is a must-read for anyone looking to master the art of peanut farming and unlock its full potential. So, whether you're a seasoned farmer or just starting out, join us on this journey to discover the incredible benefits of peanut farming with this ultimate guide.

Chapter One

Introduction to Peanut Farming

1.1 History of Peanut Farming

Peanuts, scientifically known as Arachis hypogaea, have a rich and fascinating history that dates back thousands of years. Originating in South America, these small legumes eventually made their way across continents, forever changing the agricultural landscape and becoming a staple crop in many regions of the world.

Ancient Origins and Cultivation

The story of peanut farming begins in the pre-Columbian era, where evidence suggests that peanuts were cultivated in the regions that now encompass present-day Bolivia and Peru as early as 7,600 years ago. Native indigenous groups, such as the Moche people in Peru and the Tiahuanaco people in Bolivia, recognized the nutritional value of peanuts and incorporated them into their diets.

Introduction to Africa

Peanuts were introduced to Africa during the transatlantic slave trade, which brought African people to the Americas as forced labourers. Africans, who were familiar with the cultivation of peanuts, recognized their potential as a valuable and nutritious crop. They brought this knowledge back to Africa, leading to the widespread cultivation of peanuts across the continent. Peanuts quickly found a home in various African cuisines, becoming an essential ingredient in many traditional dishes.

Arrival in Europe

European explorers, most notably Christopher Columbus, encountered peanuts during their voyages to the Americas. Peanuts were brought back to Europe, where they gained popularity as an exotic novelty. Initially seen as a delicacy, the cultivation of peanuts as a major crop in Europe did not occur until much later. However, their introduction to European markets laid the foundation for their global popularity in the coming centuries.

Growth in the United States

Peanuts arrived in the United States through African slaves who had retained their knowledge of peanut farming. However, it wasn't until the early 19th century that commercial peanut farming took root in the U.S. The American South, with its favorable climate and fertile soil, became a major hub for peanut production. Prominent figures such as George Washington Carver played a crucial role in promoting peanuts as a viable crop and pioneering various uses for peanuts beyond food, including peanut oil, peanut butter, and peanut-based products.

Modern Peanut Farming

In the modern era, peanut farming has seen significant advancements in cultivation techniques, disease resistance, and breeding programs. With improved farming practices and technology, peanut yields have increased dramatically, making peanuts a highly profitable crop for farmers around the world. Today, top peanut-producing countries include China, India, the United States, and several African nations.

1.2 Importance of Peanuts in Agriculture

Peanuts are an incredibly important crop in agriculture and play a significant role in global food security, economic sustainability, and environmental conservation. From their versatile uses to the nutritional value they offer, peanuts have earned their place as a valuable and essential crop across the world. In this section, we will take a closer look at the many ways that peanuts contribute to agriculture and our daily lives.

Versatile Uses

One of the most remarkable things about peanuts is their versatility in the kitchen. They can be roasted, boiled, fried, mashed, ground, and even made into oil or butter. Peanuts can be used in a wide variety of dishes, including desserts, sauces, salads, and snacks. Their many uses make them an essential ingredient in countless recipes around the world, and their popularity shows no signs of slowing down.

Nutritional Value

Peanuts are an excellent source of protein, fibre, and healthy fats, making them a highly nutritious food. They also contain valuable vitamins and minerals, including niacin, folate, magnesium, and vitamin E. Consuming peanuts can help promote heart health, lower cholesterol, and reduce the risk of type 2 diabetes and other chronic illnesses. For people in areas where food insecurity is a concern, peanuts can serve as an affordable and readily available source of essential nutrients.

Sustainable Agriculture

Peanuts are a hardy and resilient crop that requires fewer resources than other crops such as soy or corn. They can grow in a variety of soil types and climates, making them an ideal crop choice for areas that are prone to drought or other weather-related challenges. Additionally, peanuts can fix nitrogen in the soil, which reduces the need for synthetic fertilizers, making them a sustainable crop choice that benefits both farmers and the environment.

Economic Significance

Peanuts are a major cash crop for farmers, particularly in regions where they are a vital part of the economy. The cultivation and trade of peanuts contribute significantly to local and global economies, providing employment opportunities and income for farmers and their families. Additionally, peanut production generates revenue for companies in the food industry and supports downstream industries such as processing, packaging, and distribution.

1.3 Growth Habit and Cultivation Requirements

Peanuts, scientifically known as Arachis hypogaea, are warm-weather crops that require specific growing conditions to thrive. Understanding the growth habit and cultivation requirements of peanuts is essential for successful peanut farming. In this section, we will explore the various factors involved in cultivating peanuts, including climate, soil conditions, planting techniques, and maintenance practices.

Climate Requirements

Peanuts thrive in warm climates with temperatures ranging from 75 to 85 degrees Fahrenheit (24 to 30 degrees Celsius). They require a frost-free growing season of about 4 to 5 months. Ideally, peanuts should receive full sun exposure for most of the day. However, in extremely hot regions, partial shade during the hottest part of the day can help protect the plants from heat stress. In areas with short growing seasons, it is important to select early-maturing peanut varieties to ensure a successful harvest.

Soil Conditions

Peanuts prefer well-draining, sandy loam soils with a pH range of 5.8 to 7.2. The soil should be adequately aerated to avoid waterlogging, as excessive moisture can lead to disease and root rot. Additionally, the soil should be free of rocks, debris, and weeds that can hinder plant development. Prior to planting, it is recommended to conduct a soil test to determine nutrient deficiencies and adjust soil pH if necessary. Adequate levels of phosphorus, potassium, and other essential micronutrients are vital for healthy peanut growth.

Planting Techniques

Peanuts can be planted either through direct seeding or transplanting seedlings. Direct seeding involves planting peanut seeds directly into the prepared soil, while transplanting involves growing seedlings in a nursery and then transplanting them into the field. Regardless of the method chosen, it is important to select high-quality, certified peanut seeds to ensure optimal germination and plant health.

When planting peanuts, it is advisable to space the seeds or seedlings at a distance of about 6 to 8 inches (15 to 20 centimeters) apart within rows. The rows should be spaced around 24 to 36 inches (60 to 90 centimeters) apart to allow sufficient room for plant development and easy maintenance activities such as weeding and harvesting. Planting peanuts in a well-organized pattern promotes efficient plant growth and increases overall productivity.

Maintenance Practices

Weed control is crucial in peanut farming, as competition from weeds can reduce crop yields. Regular scouting and removal of weeds can be done manually or through the use of herbicides. However, caution should be exercised when using herbicides to avoid damage to the peanut plants. Additionally, maintaining proper soil moisture is important, especially during the critical stages of flowering and pod development. Irrigation can be necessary in regions where rainfall is irregular or insufficient for consistent peanut growth.

To prevent pest and disease infestations, it is advisable to implement integrated pest management strategies. This might include monitoring for pests and diseases, applying organic or chemical treatments when necessary, and practicing crop rotation to minimize the buildup of pathogens. It is also important to harvest peanuts at the right time when the plants have reached maturity, typically indicated by yellowing leaves and brown pods. Timely and careful harvesting is crucial to maximize yield and mitigate post-harvest losses.

Chapter Two

Preparing for Peanut Farming

2.1 Selecting the Right Land for Peanut Farming

Selecting the right land is a crucial step in preparing for peanut farming. The success of your peanut crop depends heavily on the quality and suitability of the land you choose. In this section, we will discuss important factors to consider when selecting land for peanut farming, including soil type, drainage, fertility, and previous land use.

Soil Type

Peanuts thrive in well-draining sandy loam soils. Soil with good drainage is essential to prevent waterlogging, which can lead to diseases and root rot. Sandy soils are ideal for peanuts as they promote the growth of healthy, straight roots and allow for easy peg penetration during pod development. However, it is important to note that excessive sand content can lead to nutrient leaching and reduced water-holding capacity. Therefore, a balance between sand and organic matter content is desirable for optimal peanut growth.

Drainage

Good drainage is crucial for peanut farming. Excess water can be detrimental to peanut plants, causing disease, reduced growth, and poor pod development. Avoid selecting land with poor drainage or low-lying areas prone to flooding. If possible, consider land with a gentle slope to allow for proper water runoff and prevent water accumulation.

Soil Fertility

Soil fertility plays a vital role in the success of any crop, including peanuts. Conduct a soil test before planting to determine the nutrient status of the soil and identify any deficiencies that need to be addressed. Peanuts require adequate levels of phosphorus, potassium, and other essential micronutrients for optimal growth. Incorporating organic matter into the soil can improve fertility and enhance soil structure, promoting healthier peanut plants.

Previous Land Use

Consider the previous use of the land before embarking on peanut farming. Avoid selecting land that has been heavily contaminated by chemicals or pesticides from previous agricultural practices. Contaminated soil can have negative effects on peanut growth and can potentially harm consumers. Opt for land that has been fallow or used for crops with minimal potential for disease transmission to reduce the risk of pest and disease infestations.

Access to Water and Irrigation

Adequate water supply is essential for peanut farming, especially in regions with irregular rainfall patterns. Consider the accessibility to water sources such as rivers, wells, or irrigation systems when selecting land. Having a reliable irrigation system can help ensure a consistent water supply during critical stages of peanut growth, such as flowering and pod development.

2.2 Soil Preparation and Nutrient Management

Proper soil preparation and nutrient management are crucial steps in preparing for peanut farming. Creating the ideal growing conditions for peanuts through effective soil preparation and nutrient management can significantly impact the growth, yield, and overall health of the crop. In this section, we will discuss important considerations and practices for soil preparation and nutrient management in peanut farming.

Soil Testing and Analysis

Before starting the peanut farming process, it is essential to conduct a thorough soil test. Soil testing provides valuable information about the nutrient content and pH levels of the soil, allowing farmers to make informed decisions regarding fertilizer application. By understanding the specific nutrient needs of the soil, farmers can develop a nutrient management plan tailored to the requirements of their peanut crop. Soil testing should be done well in advance to allow time for any necessary soil amendments before planting.

Soil pH Adjustment

Peanuts thrive in slightly acidic soil, with an optimal pH range between 5.8 and 7.2. If the soil's pH is outside this range, it is important to adjust it accordingly. Soil pH can be modified by adding lime to raise the pH or elemental sulfur to lower it. By maintaining the appropriate pH levels, nutrients in the soil become more available to the plants, promoting proper growth and development.

Organic Matter Incorporation

Incorporating organic matter into the soil is beneficial for several reasons. Organic matter improves soil structure, enhances water-holding capacity, and promotes nutrient retention. It also stimulates microbial activity, which aids in nutrient cycling and overall soil health. Typically, organic matter can be added to the soil through the incorporation of compost, well-rotted manure, or cover crops. Before incorporating organic matter, ensure that it is fully decomposed to prevent potential nutrient imbalances or the introduction of weed seeds.

Nutrient Application

Peanuts have specific nutrient requirements for optimal growth and yield. The primary nutrients required by peanuts are nitrogen (N), phosphorus (P), and potassium (K). The recommended application rates of these nutrients vary depending on the soil test results and the specific nutrient needs of the peanut crop. It is important to follow the nutrient management plan developed after soil testing, as over or under application of nutrients can have adverse effects on the crop and the environment.

Nitrogen is essential for vegetative growth, while phosphorus promotes root development and flowering. Potassium enhances overall plant vigour, disease resistance, and pod development. Apart from these primary nutrients, adequate levels of secondary and micronutrients, such as calcium, magnesium, sulphur, zinc, and boron, are also important for peanut health. Depending on the soil test results, additional nutrients may need to be applied through fertilizers to meet the crop's requirements.

Fertilizer Application Techniques

Fertilizer application techniques play a crucial role in ensuring efficient nutrient uptake and minimizing nutrient losses. Broadcasting or top-dressing fertilizers evenly across the field is a common practice. However, for peanuts, it is important to concentrate the fertilizers in bands or rows where the peanuts will be planted. This method, known as "banding," ensures that the nutrients are readily available to the developing roots. Additionally, side-dressing during the growing season can provide a supplemental nutrient supply to support peanut growth and yield.

2.3 Proper Irrigation Techniques

Proper irrigation techniques play a critical role in preparing for peanut farming. Adequate water supply is essential for peanut plants, especially during crucial growth stages such as flowering and pod development. Implementing effective irrigation practices can ensure consistent water availability, promote optimal plant growth, and maximize peanut yield. In this section, we will discuss important considerations and techniques for proper irrigation in peanut farming.

Water Requirements

Understanding the water requirements of peanuts is essential for efficient irrigation. Peanut plants have different water needs depending on their growth stage. During the early growth stage, peanuts require sufficient moisture to establish healthy root systems. The flowering and pod development stages are critical periods when adequate water supply is crucial to support pod growth and fill. Water stress during these stages can lead to reduced pod yield and quality.

Soil Moisture Monitoring

Monitoring soil moisture levels is essential for effective irrigation management. Various tools and techniques can help farmers determine when and how much to irrigate. Soil moisture sensors, tensiometers, and visual inspection of soil moisture are commonly used methods. By regularly monitoring soil moisture, farmers can understand the water-holding capacity of their soil and make informed decisions about irrigation scheduling.

Irrigation Scheduling

Developing an appropriate irrigation schedule is vital for peanut farming. It is important to provide water when the plants need it and avoid under- or over-irrigation. A well-planned schedule will consider factors such as soil type, crop growth stage, weather conditions, and evapotranspiration rates. Evapotranspiration is the combined loss of water through plant transpiration and soil evaporation. Efficient irrigation scheduling ensures that peanut plants receive the right amount of water at the right time, minimizing water waste and optimizing crop growth.

Irrigation Methods

Different irrigation methods can be employed in peanut farming, depending on the resources available and the characteristics of the farm. Some common irrigation techniques include:

1. Sprinkler Irrigation: Sprinkler systems distribute water over the field as a spray, simulating natural rainfall. This method provides uniform coverage and can be suitable for fields with uniform peanut plant spacing. However, it may result in water loss through evaporation and wind drift.

2. Drip Irrigation: Drip irrigation involves delivering water directly to the root zone of the plants through a network of tubes or emitters. This method reduces water wastage and allows for precise control over water application. Drip irrigation is particularly effective in sandy soils, as it provides water directly to the roots and minimizes surface evaporation.

3. Furrow Irrigation: Furrow irrigation is a traditional method where shallow channels are created between the crop rows. Water is allowed to flow through these furrows, infiltrating the soil and

providing moisture to the plants. Although furrow irrigation may result in some water loss through runoff, it can be a cost-effective option for peanut farming.

Water Conservation Techniques

Water conservation practices should be incorporated into peanut farming to reduce water usage and promote sustainable agriculture. Some techniques for water conservation include:

1. Mulching: Applying organic or synthetic mulch around peanut plants helps reduce soil moisture evaporation, keeping the soil moist and reducing water loss.

2. Cover Crops: Planting cover crops during the off-season can help improve soil health and moisture retention. These crops act as a protective

layer, reducing evaporation and enriching the soil with organic matter.

3. Irrigation Scheduling Based on Crop needs: Align irrigation scheduling with the crop's growth stage and weather conditions to avoid overwatering and unnecessary water waste.

4. Irrigation System Maintenance: Regularly inspect and maintain irrigation equipment to ensure proper functioning and prevent water leakage and inefficiencies.

2.4 Seed Selection and Treatment

Seed selection and treatment are vital steps in preparing for peanut farming. Choosing high-quality seeds and properly treating them can significantly impact the success of the crop. Optimal seed selection ensures that the planting material has desirable traits, while seed treatment helps protect against diseases, pests, and other potential threats. In this section, we will discuss important considerations for seed selection and treatment in peanut farming.

Seed Selection

Selecting the right seed is the foundation of a successful peanut crop. Essential factors to consider when selecting peanut seeds include:

1. Variety Selection: Choose peanut varieties that are well-suited to your specific growing region, considering factors such as climate, soil type, and disease resistance. Different peanut varieties have varying characteristics, such as growth habits, maturity, and yield potential. Research and consult with local agricultural extension services to determine the most suitable varieties for your farm.

2. Quality Assurance: Ensure that the seeds you select have undergone proper quality assurance processes. This involves checking for purity, germination rates, and freedom from diseases. Seeds should be free from impurities, have high germination rates, and comply with national seed laws and regulations.

3. Yield Potential: Consider the yield potential of the selected peanut seeds. Look for varieties that have a history of high yields and are known to perform well under similar growing conditions. It is also important to consider market demand for the peanut variety you choose.

4. Disease Resistance: Select peanut varieties that have resistance to prevalent diseases in your area. Disease-resistant varieties can help reduce the risk of yield loss due to diseases, ultimately improving the overall health and productivity of the crop.

Seed Treatment

Seed treatment is an essential step in protecting peanut crops from seed-borne diseases, pests, and other potential threats. Here are some common seed treatment methods:

1. Fungicide Treatment: Seeds can be treated with fungicides to protect against fungal diseases that may be present on or within the seed. Fungicide treatment can help prevent damping-off, root rot, and other seed-borne fungal diseases. Ensure that the fungicide used is labelled for peanut seed treatment and follow the recommended application rates.

2. Insecticide Treatment: Peanuts are vulnerable to various insect pests, including seedling pests and soil-borne insects. Treating the seeds with insecticides can help protect against pests such as

thrips, wireworms, and nematodes. Again, make sure to use insecticides labelled for peanut seed treatment and follow the recommended application guidelines.

3. Biological Seed Treatment: Biological seed treatments involve the use of beneficial microorganisms to protect seeds from diseases and promote healthy plant growth. Certain strains of bacteria and fungi can help suppress harmful pathogens and enhance nutrient availability, ultimately improving plant health.

4. Seed Disinfection: Seeds can be disinfected using methods such as hot water treatment or chemical treatment. These treatments help eliminate potential pathogens that may be present on the seed surface, reducing the risk of diseases during germination and early growth stages.

Seed Storage

Proper seed storage is crucial to maintain seed quality and viability. Store peanut seeds in cool, dry, and well-ventilated areas to prevent moisture buildup and the growth of fungi. Use appropriate containers, such as breathable bags or dry storage bins, to allow air circulation and prevent condensation. Regularly check stored seeds for any signs of moisture or pest damage and discard any damaged or compromised seeds.

Chapter Three

Planting and Growing Peanuts

3.1 Best Time for Planting Peanuts

Choosing the right time for planting peanuts is crucial for their successful growth and development. Peanuts have specific temperature and moisture requirements that determine the optimal planting window. By understanding the best time for planting peanuts, farmers can optimize crop yield and minimize potential risks. In this section, we will discuss important considerations for timing peanut planting and growing.

Climate Considerations

The climate of a particular region plays a significant role in determining the best time for planting peanuts. Peanuts thrive in warm and humid conditions. They require a frost-free growing season with optimal temperatures between 70°F to 90°F (21°C to 32°C) for successful growth. It is important to consider the length of the growing season and the average temperatures in your region before deciding on the planting date.

Soil Temperature and Moisture

Soil temperature and moisture are critical factors to consider when determining the best time for planting peanuts. Peanut seeds require a minimum soil temperature of 65°F (18°C) for germination. Planting peanuts when the soil has reached the desired temperature ensures quick and uniform emergence of seedlings.

In addition to soil temperature, adequate soil moisture is essential for successful peanut germination and establishment. Planting peanuts during periods of adequate soil moisture can help ensure sufficient water availability for seedling emergence and early growth. It is advisable to avoid planting peanuts during excessively wet or dry periods, as this can negatively impact germination and plant development.

Growing Season Length

The length of the growing season is an important consideration for peanut planting. Peanuts typically require a growing season of 120 to 150 days, depending on the variety and growing conditions. It is crucial to select peanut varieties that are suitable for the available growing season length in your region. Shorter-season varieties may be more appropriate for areas with shorter growing seasons, while longer-season varieties may be suitable for regions with extended frost-free periods.

Rotations and Crop Calendar

Crop rotations and a well-thought-out crop calendar can also influence the timing of peanut planting. It is advisable to rotate peanut crops with non-peanut crops to minimize the build-up of diseases, pests, and weeds that specifically target peanuts. Plan crop rotations in such a way that it allows for adequate time between peanut crops to ensure disease and pest pressure is minimized.

A crop calendar can help farmers plan and space out their planting activities. It takes into account factors such as the length of the growing season, frost dates, and the cropping sequence. A well-designed crop calendar ensures that peanuts are planted at the optimal time, taking into consideration the specific requirements of the crop and the rotations planned for the season.

Local Agro-advisories and Expertise

Consulting local agro-advisories and seeking expert advice can provide valuable insights into the best time for planting peanuts in your specific region. Local agricultural extension services and experts are familiar with the climatic conditions, soil types, and pest and disease risks in your area. They can provide guidance on the ideal planting window and recommend suitable peanut varieties based on local conditions.

3.2 Planting Methods: In-Row and Between-Row Spacing

Proper planting methods are essential for the successful growth and development of peanuts. In-row and between-row spacing are key considerations when deciding how to plant peanuts. These spacing techniques impact factors such as plant population, weed control, disease management, and overall crop yield. In this section, we will discuss the advantages and considerations of in-row and between-row spacing for planting and growing peanuts.

In-Row Spacing

In-row spacing refers to the distance between individual peanut plants within a row. The optimal in-row spacing for peanuts depends on various factors, including variety selection, soil type, irrigation practices, and equipment used.

1. Plant Population and Yields: Planting peanuts with the proper in-row spacing can help maximize plant population and ultimately increase crop yields. However, planting peanuts too close together can lead to crowded plants, limited air circulation, and increased disease pressure. On the other hand, wider in-row spacing may allow for improved plant

airflow, higher pod penetration during harvesting, and reduced shading.

2. Weed Control: Effective weed control is crucial for peanut crop productivity. In-row spacing plays a role in managing weeds. Wider in-row spacing allows more room for cultivating and mechanical weed control, while narrower in-row spacing can promote faster canopy closure, reducing weed competition.

3. Equipment and Farming Practices: In-row spacing should be adjusted based on the equipment used for planting, cultivation, and harvesting. Consider the equipment size and capabilities when determining the appropriate in-row spacing. Properly spaced rows allow for efficient machinery maneuverability and minimize potential damage to plants and pods during mechanical operations.

Between-Row Spacing

Between-row spacing refers to the distance between adjacent rows of peanut plants. This spacing impacts plant growth, canopy development, and overall crop management.

1. Canopy Development: Peanut plants require enough space between rows to allow for proper canopy development. Adequate between-row spacing allows plants to attain their full potential in terms of leaf area, root development, and pod yield.

2. Penetration and Harvesting Efficiency: Appropriate between-row spacing facilitates better access for farm machinery during cultivation, pest management, and harvesting. Wide enough spacing ensures proper penetration of machinery for effective operations and minimizes damage to peanut plants and pods during harvesting.

3. Disease Management: Proper between-row spacing contributes to increased air circulation and reduced humidity within the plant canopy. This can help minimize the risk of fungal diseases, such as leaf spot, as well as improve pesticide penetration during disease management.

Considerations for Optimal Spacing

Determining the optimal in-row and between-row spacing depends on various factors, including:

1. Variety: Different peanut varieties may have specific recommendations for spacing based on their growth habit, branching pattern, and yield potential. Seek guidance from seed suppliers or agricultural experts for variety-specific recommendations.

2. Soil and Irrigation: Soil type and irrigation practices play a role in determining spacing requirements.

Factors such as water-holding capacity, nutrient availability, and drainage are crucial considerations. Ensure proper irrigation management to avoid excessive or inadequate moisture levels in relation to the chosen spacing.

3. Equipment and Operational Efficiency: Consider the size and capabilities of your farming equipment when selecting spacing. Ensuring compatibility between the chosen spacing and machinery will help maximize operational efficiency and minimize potential damage to plants and pods during mechanical operations.

4. Weed and Pest Control: Spacing decisions should also consider the weed and pest control methods employed, whether chemical, mechanical, or a combination of both. Wider spacing allows for more effective mechanical weed control, while narrower spacing may benefit from herbicide applications.

3.3 Nutrient Requirements During Growth

When it comes to growing peanuts, proper nutrient management is essential for a successful crop. Peanuts have specific nutrient requirements for their growth and development. Adequate nutrients, both macronutrients such as nitrogen, phosphorus, and potassium, and micronutrients such as zinc, iron, and manganese, ensure optimal peanut yield and quality. In this section, we will discuss the nutrient requirements during growth for planting and growing peanuts.

Nutrient Requirements During Growth

The nutrient requirements for peanuts vary depending on the growth stage. Each growth stage has different nutrient demands that must be met to maximize yield potential and quality. The following are the key nutrient requirements of peanuts throughout the different growth stages:

Vegetative Stage

The vegetative stage is the initial phase of peanut growth, and it lasts for about 35-40 days after planting. During this stage, peanut plants require adequate nitrogen (N), phosphorus (P), and potassium (K) for root development and vegetative growth. Nitrogen is essential for the synthesis of chlorophyll, which is critical for photosynthesis, while phosphorus improves root growth, and potassium helps with fruit development and water-use efficiency.

Reproductive Stage

The reproductive stage of peanut growth begins shortly after the vegetative stage and lasts until the end of the growing season. During this stage, peanut plants have a high demand for nutrients, especially potassium, which is essential for pod filling and quality. Calcium is also essential during this stage for pod development and disease control, while phosphorus and nitrogen are necessary for stalk strength, healthy foliage, and maintaining pod size.

Nutrient Deficiencies

Nutrient deficiencies can negatively impact peanut yield and plant quality. Common nutrient deficiencies in peanuts include:

1. Nitrogen: Nitrogen deficiency results in stunted plants with yellowish-green leaves, reduced pod formation, and lower yields.

2. Phosphorus: Phosphorus deficiency causes poor root growth, smaller leaves, and reduced pod formation.

3. Potassium: Potassium deficiency results in smaller pods with poor filling, weak plant growth, yellowing of leaves, and increased susceptibility to disease.

4. Micronutrients: Micronutrient deficiencies can occur in peanuts and can cause various symptoms such as leaves with chlorosis and marginal necrosis.

Nutrient Application

To meet the nutrient requirements of peanuts, it is important to apply fertilizers appropriately. Soil testing is a valuable tool to help ensure adequate nutrient availability. Soil testing can help identify nutrient imbalances, allowing for the implementation of appropriate nutrient application rates.

Various fertiliser application methods are available to meet peanut nutrient requirements. The following are a few common methods:

1. Broadcast Application: Applying fertilizers to the soil surface is called broadcast application. It is a common method for phosphorus and potassium fertilizers.

2. Banded Application: This involves placing fertilizers close to the plant rootzone. Banded application allows for more efficient use of fertilizer, and it is especially useful for nitrogen fertilizers.

3. Foliar Application: Foliar application involves the application of liquid fertilizers directly to the leaves. This method is useful for micronutrient deficiencies.

3.4 Pest and Disease Management

Pests and diseases can significantly impact the growth and productivity of peanut crops. Effective pest and disease management strategies are crucial for successful peanut planting and growing. By implementing preventive measures, monitoring techniques, and appropriate control methods, farmers can mitigate the risks associated with pests and diseases. In this section, we will discuss the importance of pest and disease management and various strategies that can be employed.

Importance of Pest and Disease Management

Peanuts are vulnerable to a variety of pests and diseases throughout their growth cycle. These pests can include insects such as aphids, thrips, and caterpillars, while diseases can range from fungal infections like early leaf spot and late leaf spot to viral diseases. Left unmanaged, pests and diseases can cause yield losses, reduced crop quality, and even complete crop failure. Therefore, it is vital to adopt proper pest and disease management practices to protect peanut crops.

Pest Management Strategies

Successful pest management involves a combination of integrated pest management (IPM) approaches, including cultural, biological, and chemical control methods. Here are some strategies for managing pests in peanut crops:

1. Crop Rotation: Implementing a crop rotation system can help break pest cycles and reduce pest pressure. Growing peanuts in a rotation with other crops disrupts the habitat and food source of pests, reducing their chances of survival and reproduction.

2. Resistant Varieties: Planting peanut varieties that are resistant or tolerant to specific pests can provide a natural defence mechanism. Consult seed suppliers or agricultural experts for recommendations on pest-resistant peanut varieties.

3. Monitoring and Scouting: Regular monitoring and scouting of peanut fields are essential to detect pest populations at early stages. Trained agronomists or agricultural extension specialists can help identify pests and determine appropriate control measures based on population thresholds.

4. Biological Control: Beneficial insects, such as ladybugs and lacewings, can help control pest populations naturally. Encouraging the presence of these beneficial insects by providing suitable habitats, such as flowering plants, can enhance biological control.

5. Chemical Control: When necessary, judicious use of insecticides or acaricides can be employed to manage pests. It is important to follow recommended application rates, timings, and safety

precautions to minimize any negative impacts on non-target organisms and the environment.

Disease Management Strategies

Disease management in peanut crops is crucial for maintaining healthy plants and ensuring optimal yield. Here are some disease management strategies for peanut crops:

1. Crop Rotation: Similarly to pest management, crop rotation can help reduce disease pressure by interrupting disease cycles. Avoid planting peanuts in the same field consecutively to minimize the buildup of soil-borne pathogens.

2. Resistant Varieties: Planting peanut varieties with genetic resistance to specific diseases can help minimize disease incidence and severity. Consult

with seed suppliers to select varieties with desired disease resistance traits.

3. Sanitation Practices: Proper field and equipment sanitation can help prevent the introduction and spread of diseases. Cleaning and disinfecting equipment, removing crop debris, and practicing good hygiene can reduce the chances of disease transmission.

4. Fungicides: In cases where diseases are present or have a history of occurrence, strategic use of fungicides may be necessary. Follow label instructions and consult with agricultural experts to determine appropriate fungicide applications based on disease presence and severity.

5. Irrigation Management: Proper irrigation management can help minimize disease incidence, particularly foliar diseases. Avoid overwatering and ensure proper drainage to maintain optimal soil

moisture levels and prevent conditions favourable for disease development.

Chapter Four

Crop Care and Maintenance

4.1 Weed Control Strategies

Weeds are unwanted plants that can compete with crops for resources such as sunlight, water, and nutrients. Managing weeds is crucial for crop care and maintenance, as they can significantly reduce crop yields and quality. Implementing effective weed control strategies can help farmers maintain clean and healthy crop fields. In this section, we will discuss the importance of weed control and various strategies that can be employed.

Importance of Weed Control

Weed control is essential for several reasons:

1. Nutrient Competition: Weeds compete with crops for essential nutrients, resulting in nutrient

deficiencies and stunted growth. By controlling weeds, crops can receive the necessary nutrients for optimal development.

2. Water Competition: Weeds can absorb significant amounts of water, depleting soil moisture that crops require for growth. Effective weed control ensures that crops receive adequate water for their needs.

3. Sunlight Interference: Weeds can shade crops, limiting their access to sunlight. As a result, crops may experience reduced photosynthesis and lower yields. Controlling weeds allows crops to receive sufficient sunlight for their growth.

4. Disease and Pest Harborage: Weeds can host pests and diseases that can spread to nearby crops. Proper weed control minimizes the potential for pest and disease infestations, helping to maintain crop health.

Weed Control Strategies

Successful weed control involves a combination of preventive, cultural, mechanical, and chemical control methods. Here are some strategies for managing weeds in crop fields:

1. Crop Rotation: Implementing a crop rotation system disrupts the lifecycle of weeds. Different crops may have different weed species or timing requirements, making it difficult for weed populations to establish and reproduce.

2. Mulching: Applying organic or synthetic mulch around plants helps suppress weed growth by blocking sunlight to the soil surface. Mulching also helps retain soil moisture and regulates soil temperature, promoting healthier crop growth.

3. Cover Crops: Planting cover crops during the off-season can help smother weeds and improve soil health. Cover crops compete with weeds for

resources and provide a physical barrier against weed establishment.

4. Mechanical Control: Hand weeding, hoeing, or using mechanical weeders can physically remove or disrupt weed growth. Mechanical control is effective for removing individual weeds or controlling weeds in smaller areas.

5. Herbicides: Herbicides are chemical compounds specifically designed to control weeds. They can be selective or non-selective, targeting specific weed species or a broad range of weeds, respectively. Herbicides should be used judiciously, following label instructions and considering potential impacts on non-target plants and the environment.

6. Integrated Weed Management (IWM): IWM involves integrating multiple weed control strategies to create a comprehensive approach. By combining cultural practices, mechanical methods, and

targeted herbicide use, IWM maximizes weed control effectiveness while minimizing reliance on a single control method.

7. Timely Weed Control: Early weed control is crucial to prevent weed competition and minimize the weed seedbank in the soil. Regular monitoring and timely action are necessary to effectively manage weed populations throughout the growing season.

4.2 Fertilizer Application and Management

Fertilizers are essential to crop care and maintenance as they provide the necessary nutrients for optimal growth and yield. However, improper fertilizer application and management can have negative impacts on both crop health and the environment. Effective fertilizer management involves understanding the nutrient needs of the crops, selecting appropriate fertilizers, and applying them in a way that maximizes their benefits while minimizing potential risks. In this section, we will discuss the importance of fertilizer application and management and various strategies that can be employed.

Importance of Fertilizer Application and Management

Fertilizers provide essential nutrients that are necessary for crops to grow healthy and productive. These nutrients include nitrogen, phosphorus, potassium, calcium, magnesium, and other trace elements. Applying fertilizers in the right amounts and at the right time can improve crop growth, yield, and quality. However, excessive use of fertilizers can lead to nutrient imbalances, soil acidification, and environmental pollution. Therefore, it is essential to manage fertilizers properly to achieve optimal crop benefits while minimizing risks.

Fertilizer Application and Management Strategies

Successful fertilizer application and management involve a combination of approaches, including soil testing, nutrient management planning, fertilizer selection, application timing, and placement. Here are some strategies for managing fertilizers in crop fields:

1. Soil Testing: Soil testing is crucial for determining the nutrient requirements of crops and developing an appropriate nutrient management plan. Soil tests provide information on soil pH, organic matter content, and nutrient levels, allowing farmers to adjust fertilizer application rates and timing accordingly.

2. Nutrient Management Planning: A nutrient management plan outlines the crop nutrient requirements, fertilizer application rates and timing, and other practices, such as crop rotation, to

optimize nutrient use efficiency and minimize environmental impacts. A nutrient management plan also helps farmers comply with local regulations on fertilizer use.

3. Fertilizer Selection: Selecting fertilizers with appropriate nutrient ratios and formulations based on crop needs and soil test results is critical for effective nutrient management. Organic fertilizers, such as compost and manure, can also provide significant soil nutrients and improve soil health.

4. Application Timing: Applying fertilizers at the appropriate time, according to crop growth stages and nutrient requirements, is essential for maximizing nutrient use efficiency and minimizing nutrient loss. Proper timing can also prevent fertilizer run-off, leaching, and volatilization, reducing environmental impacts.

5. Fertilizer Placement: Placing fertilizers in the right location can improve nutrient uptake and minimize potential losses. For example, placing fertilizers close to the root zone, in bands, or below the soil surface can improve nutrient availability and reduce exposure to weathering, volatilization, and leaching.

6. Irrigation Management: Proper irrigation management can enhance fertilizer uptake by crops. Irrigation systems such as drip, furrow, or sprinkler can help deliver water and nutrients to crops in a targeted and efficient manner.

7. Use of Technologies: Technology solutions such as precision agriculture can help optimize fertilizer application and management. Sensors, remote sensing, and GPS mapping can aid farmers in making informed decisions on fertilizer application rates and timing based on crop needs and soil variability.

4.3 Watering Techniques During the Growing Season

Water is a vital resource for crop growth and development. During the growing season, proper watering techniques are crucial for crop care and maintenance, as they ensure that crops receive adequate moisture for optimal growth and yield. However, improper watering practices can lead to water wastage, nutrient leaching, and crop stress. In this section, we will discuss the importance of watering techniques and various strategies that can be employed for efficient water management in crop fields.

Importance of Watering Techniques

Water plays a critical role in various plant processes, including nutrient uptake, photosynthesis, and cell expansion. Adequate water supply ensures that crops can develop healthy root systems, assimilate nutrients, and produce the required amount of leaf area for effective photosynthesis. Insufficient water can lead to crop stress, reduced growth, and yield loss. On the other hand, overwatering can saturate the soil, restrict root respiration, and promote the development of diseases. Therefore, optimizing watering techniques is essential for maintaining crop health and maximizing productivity.

Watering Techniques for Efficient Water Management

Efficient water management involves understanding the water requirements of crops, monitoring soil moisture levels, and employing appropriate watering techniques. Here are some strategies for watering crops during the growing season:

1. Monitoring Soil Moisture: Regularly monitoring soil moisture is crucial for determining when crops require irrigation. Techniques such as soil sampling, tensiometers, and moisture sensors can provide

accurate information on soil moisture levels, allowing farmers to make informed decisions about irrigation timing and amount.

2. Irrigation Scheduling: Following a systematic irrigation schedule can help ensure that crops receive water at optimal times. Factors such as crop growth stage, soil type, weather conditions, and water-holding capacity influence the frequency and duration of irrigation events.

3. Drip Irrigation: Drip irrigation is an efficient method that delivers water directly to the root zone of plants. It minimizes water loss due to evaporation and runoff, improves nutrient uptake, and reduces weed growth. Drip irrigation systems can be automated and tailored to meet the specific water needs of different crops.

4. Mulching: Applying organic or synthetic mulch around plants helps conserve soil moisture by reducing evaporation and weed competition. Mulching also regulates soil temperature, improves soil structure, and protects against erosion. Mulch can be especially beneficial in areas with limited water resources.

5. Sprinkler Irrigation: Sprinkler irrigation is a widely used technique that distributes water through overhead sprinklers. It provides uniform coverage and can be suitable for large-scale crop production. However, care must be taken to prevent excessive water evaporation and disease development.

6. Proper Irrigation Timing: Watering crops at the right time of the day can enhance water uptake and minimize evaporation losses. It is generally recommended to irrigate early in the morning or

late in the evening to avoid high evaporation rates during peak sunlight hours.

7. Implementing Water Conservation Practices: Adopting water conservation practices can be beneficial in areas where water resources are limited or drought conditions prevail. Practices such as rainwater harvesting, precision irrigation, and deficit irrigation can help optimise water use, minimize wastage, and ensure the sustainability of water resources.

4.4 Disease Prevention and Control Measures

Diseases caused by pathogens can have devastating effects on crops, leading to reduced yield and quality. Disease prevention and control measures are crucial for crop care and maintenance, as they help mitigate the risks of disease outbreaks and ensure the long-term health of crops. By implementing effective disease management strategies, farmers can minimize crop losses, increase productivity, and promote sustainable agricultural practices. In this section, we will discuss the importance of disease prevention and control measures and various strategies that can be employed.

Importance of Disease Prevention and Control Measures

Crop diseases can be caused by bacteria, fungi, viruses, and other pathogens. These pathogens can infect plants through various entry points, such as wounds, insect vectors, soil, or airborne spores. Once a disease establishes itself in a crop, it can spread rapidly and cause significant damage. Disease prevention and control measures are essential for maintaining crop health and productivity. By implementing these measures, farmers can reduce the incidence and severity of diseases, minimise the need for chemical treatments, and promote a sustainable farming system.

Disease Prevention and Control Strategies

1. Crop Rotation: Implementing crop rotation is an effective strategy for disease prevention. By rotating crops, farmers can disrupt the disease cycle, reduce pathogen buildup in the soil, and minimize the risk of recurrence. Rotating crops with plant families that are less susceptible to the same diseases can further enhance disease control.

2. Resistant Varieties: Planting resistant crop varieties can provide an effective defense against specific diseases. Resistant varieties have been bred to possess genetic traits that enable them to withstand or tolerate certain pathogens. By selecting and planting resistant varieties, farmers can reduce the need for chemical treatments and reduce disease incidence.

3. Sanitation Practices: Maintaining good sanitation practices is essential for disease prevention. Removing or destroying crop residues, weeds, and volunteer plants can eliminate potential sources of pathogens. Equipment and tools should be cleaned and disinfected regularly to prevent the spread of diseases between fields. Disease-contaminated plant debris should be properly disposed of to prevent pathogens from remaining in the field.

4. Crop Nutrition and Soil Health: Maintaining optimal soil fertility and crop nutrition can enhance plant health and disease resistance. Balanced fertilization, organic matter additions, and soil amendments can promote vigorous plant growth and strengthen the plants' natural defence mechanisms. Practices that improve soil health, such as crop rotation, cover cropping, and reduced tillage, can also contribute to disease prevention.

5. Integrated Pest Management (IPM): Adopting an IPM approach can help prevent and control diseases. IPM involves combining various strategies, such as cultural practices, biological control, and targeted chemical treatments, to manage pests and diseases in an environmentally-sustainable way. By identifying and monitoring disease risks and using appropriate control measures, farmers can effectively manage diseases while minimizing the use of pesticides.

6. Early Disease Detection: Regular scouting and monitoring for disease symptoms are crucial for early disease detection. Familiarizing oneself with common disease symptoms, such as leaf spots, wilting, discoloration, and deformities, can aid in timely intervention. Early detection allows for prompt action, such as targeted treatments or

adjustments to cultural practices, to prevent the spread of diseases.

7. Weather Monitoring: Certain diseases are favoured by specific weather conditions. Monitoring weather patterns, such as temperature, humidity, and rainfall, can help farmers anticipate disease outbreaks and take preventive actions. By understanding the disease cycle and knowing the conditions that favour pathogen development, farmers can time their disease control measures effectively.

8. Chemical Treatments: In cases where other measures are insufficient or ineffective, chemical treatments may be necessary to control diseases. When using chemical treatments, it is essential to follow label instructions, apply the correct dosage, and adhere to safety precautions to minimize

environmental impact and potential harm to beneficial organisms.

Chapter five

Harvesting and Post-Harvest Handling

5.1 Indicators for Peanut Maturity and Readiness to Harvest

Harvesting peanuts at the right stage of maturity is crucial for ensuring optimal yield and quality. Determining the correct timing for peanut harvest can be challenging, as it requires considering multiple indicators to assess the crop's readiness. By understanding the indicators for peanut maturity and employing appropriate harvesting and post-harvest handling techniques, farmers can maximize their harvest and maintain the quality of the peanuts. In this section, we will discuss the indicators for peanut maturity and readiness to harvest, as well as the best practices for harvesting and post-harvest handling.

Indicators of Peanut Maturity

1. Pod Development: Monitoring pod development is an essential indicator of peanut maturity. As peanuts mature, the pods undergo physiological changes, transitioning from a green or yellow colour to a mature tan or brown. Mature pods become tighter, and the shell colour becomes darker. The formation of pods near the base of the plant is another indication of maturity.

2. Seed Color: Peanut seeds undergo colour changes as they mature. Immature seeds are usually white or pale yellow, while mature seeds take on a more distinct tan or brown colour. The development of a brown coloration throughout the seed is a strong indicator of maturity.

3. Seed Texture: The texture of peanut seeds can also indicate maturity. Immature seeds tend to be soft

and easily damaged, while mature seeds become harder and more resistant to pressure.

4. Pod Extraction Force: The force required to separate the seeds from the pods, known as the pod extraction force, can provide a good indication of peanut maturity. As the pods mature, the seeds become more firmly attached, requiring greater force to separate them.

5. Sound Test: Another traditional method to assess peanut maturity is through the sound test. By shaking the pods, farmers can listen for a rattling or cracking sound, which indicates that the nuts are mature and well-developed within the pods.

Harvesting and Post-Harvest Handling Techniques

1. Timing: Peanut harvest timing is critical to maximize yield and quality. Harvesting too early can result in immature seeds with low yield, while delaying

harvest can lead to seed damage, disease susceptibility, and deterioration in quality. Monitoring the indicators of maturity discussed above can help determine the optimal timing.

2. Combine Harvesting: Mechanized combine harvesting is the most common method for harvesting peanuts. The equipment should be properly adjusted to minimize losses and damage to the crop. Combines equipped with appropriate picking headers and air separation systems can efficiently detach and separate the crop from the soil, vines, and excess foliage.

3. Inversion and Drying: After harvest, it is common practice to invert the peanut plants to dry them before further processing. Inverting involves lifting the entire plant and inverting it upside down to allow the peanuts to dry in the field. Once the

plants are dry, they can be mechanically harvested or picked by hand.

4. Curing: Proper curing is essential to ensure the longevity and quality of the harvested peanuts. Curing involves allowing the peanuts to dry further under controlled conditions, typically in well-ventilated structures or warehouses. This process reduces the moisture content of the peanuts, preventing mould growth and maintaining flavour and oil stability.

5. Cleaning and Grading: After curing, the peanuts need to undergo cleaning and grading processes. This involves removing foreign material, damaged or immature seeds, and separating the peanuts into different sizes and quality classes. Cleaning ensures that only high-quality peanuts are sent for further processing or market.

6. Storage: Proper storage is critical to maintaining peanut quality. Peanuts should be stored in cool, dry, and well-ventilated facilities to prevent moisture buildup and reduce the risk of mould and aflatoxin contamination. Regular inspection and monitoring of storage conditions are necessary to prevent deterioration.

5.2 Harvesting Techniques and Equipment

Harvesting is a critical stage in the agricultural production process that requires careful attention to ensure the timely and efficient collection of crops. Proper harvesting techniques and equipment are essential for minimizing crop losses, maximising yield, and maintaining the quality of the harvested produce. In this section, we will discuss various harvesting techniques, equipment options, and best practices for post-harvest handling.

Harvesting Techniques

1. Manual Harvesting: Manual harvesting involves handpicking or using handheld tools, such as knives or sickles, to cut or detach the crops from the plants. This method is commonly used for crops that are delicate or require selective harvesting, such as fruits, vegetables, and flowers. Manual harvesting allows for precise selection and reduces damage to the plants and produce.

2. Mechanical Harvesting: Mechanical harvesting is a more efficient method suitable for crops that can be mechanically detached from the plants. Mechanized harvesters, such as combine harvesters, are commonly used for crops like cereals, oilseeds, cotton, and sugarcane. These machines are designed to cut, thresh, separate, and collect the plant material or seeds in one pass.

3. Strip Harvesting: Strip harvesting involves removing the entire row or strip of crops at once, usually using a harvesting machine. This method is commonly used for crops like forage, hay, or silage, where the whole plant, including the leaves and stems, is harvested and used as feed or bedding material for livestock.

4. Selective Harvesting: In selective harvesting, only the mature or desired portions of the crop are harvested, leaving the rest to continue growing and ripening. This method is commonly used for crops like tree fruits, berries, and vineyards where not all fruits or berries ripen at the same time. Selective harvesting ensures that only ripe, high-quality produce is collected.

Harvesting Equipment

1. Combine Harvesters: Combine harvesters, also known as combine harvesters or simply combines, are versatile machines widely used for harvesting grain crops like wheat, corn, rice, and soybeans. These machines perform multiple functions, including cutting, threshing, separating, and cleaning the crop. Combine harvesters can handle large volumes of crops efficiently, improving harvesting productivity.

2. Forage Harvesters: Forage harvesters are specialized machines used for harvesting crops like grasses, maize, and sorghum for animal feed. These machines are designed to cut and chop the plant material into small pieces, making it suitable for ensiling, silage, or other forms of preservation.

3. Cotton Harvesters: Cotton harvesters are specifically designed for harvesting cotton crops.

These machines pick the cotton bolls from the plants, separate the lint from the seeds, and collect the lint for further processing. Cotton harvesters help minimize labor requirements and reduce damage to the cotton fibers.

4. Fruit Harvesters: Fruit harvesters come in various designs, depending on the type of fruit being harvested. These machines aid in fast and efficient fruit picking, thereby reducing labour costs and minimizing fruit damage. Fruit harvesters can be used for crops like apples, oranges, berries, and cherries.

5. Vegetable Harvesters: Vegetable harvesters are specialized machines used for harvesting a wide range of vegetables, including leafy greens, root crops, and vine crops. These machines assist in loosening, cutting, or uprooting the vegetables from

the plants, saving time and labour during the harvest.

Best Practices for Post-Harvest Handling

1. Handling Techniques: Proper handling techniques are crucial to minimize damage and bruising to the harvested crops. This includes careful loading, transportation, and unloading of the crops to prevent physical damage, maintain freshness, and maximize shelf life.

2. Sorting and Grading: Sorting and grading involve separating the harvested produce based on quality, size, and appearance. This process ensures consistency in the product and allows for better marketability. Automated sorting and grading machines can efficiently categorize the produce based on pre-set criteria.

3. Cleaning and Washing: Depending on the crop, cleaning and washing may be necessary to remove dirt, debris, or contaminants. This step contributes to maintaining the quality and hygiene of the produce, especially for fresh fruits and vegetables.

4. Cooling and Storage: Proper cooling and storage are essential to preserve the quality and extend the shelf life of harvested crops. Cooling techniques, such as hydro cooling or forced-air cooling, can quickly lower the temperature of the produce to reduce deterioration. Storing crops in controlled environments, such as cold rooms or refrigerated warehouses, helps maintain optimal temperature and humidity conditions.

5. Packaging and Labeling: Packaging serves as a protective barrier and a means of branding and marketing the harvested produce. Proper packaging materials and practices help prevent

physical damage and maintain freshness. Additionally, labelling the packaging with relevant information, such as the crop type, variety, harvest date, and handling instructions, assists in traceability and consumer communication.

5.3 Drying, Curing, and Storing Peanuts

Drying, curing, and storing peanuts after harvest are essential steps in the post-harvest handling process. These processes are crucial for preserving the quality of the peanuts, preventing spoilage, and maximizing their shelf life. In this section, we will discuss the proper techniques and best practices for drying, curing, and storing peanuts.

Drying Peanuts

Drying peanuts after harvest is crucial to reduce their moisture content to a safe level, inhibit mould growth, and prevent spoilage. Here are some key techniques for drying peanuts effectively:

1. Field Drying: After digging up the peanuts, they are left to dry in the field for one to two days. During this time, the peanuts should be spread out in a single layer to expose them to the sun and air, facilitating the drying process. It is crucial to monitor the weather during field drying to avoid prolonged exposure to excessive moisture or rain.

2. Mechanical Drying: Mechanical dryers can be used to speed up the drying process, especially in areas with high humidity or unfavourable weather conditions. These dryers use forced air or heated air to reduce the moisture content of the peanuts.

Care should be taken to avoid excessive heat, as it may lead to quality deterioration.

3. Moisture Monitoring: It is essential to monitor the moisture content of the peanuts during the drying process. The target moisture content may vary depending on the intended use of the peanuts, but typically, a safe range is between 8% and 10%. Moisture meters or other testing equipment can be used to ensure optimal drying.

Curing Peanuts

Curing is a critical step performed after drying to develop the flavour, improve storage quality, and enhance the colour of the peanuts. Here are some important considerations for curing peanuts:

1. Natural Curing: Natural or air curing involves allowing the peanuts to cure under ambient

conditions for a specific period, usually around three to four weeks. During this time, the peanuts undergo biochemical changes that enhance their flavour and quality.

2. Artificial Curing: Artificial curing can be used when natural curing is not feasible or to speed up the process. In artificial curing, the peanuts are subjected to controlled temperature and humidity conditions in curing barns or enclosed structures. This method allows for more precise control of the curing parameters.

Storing Peanuts

Proper storage is vital to maintain the quality and prevent spoilage of peanuts. Here are some key practices for storing peanuts:

1. Cleaning and Sorting: Before storing, it is crucial to remove any damaged, mouldy, or discoloured

peanuts. Sorting the peanuts based on size and quality can help achieve more uniform storage conditions.

2. Storage Environment: Peanuts should be stored in a cool, dry, and well-ventilated environment. The storage area should be free from pests and rodents. Temperature and humidity should be maintained within appropriate ranges to prevent mould growth and rancidity.

3. Packaging: Peanuts can be stored in jute bags, woven polypropylene bags, or vacuum-sealed bags. The packaging material should be clean and free from contaminants. Additionally, proper sealing and labelling the packages with relevant information, such as harvest date and variety, can assist in traceability and quality control.

4. Stock Rotation: Practicing stock rotation is essential to ensure that older peanuts are used or sold

before fresher batches. This helps maintain the quality of the peanuts and prevents them from becoming stale or rancid.

5.4 Quality Assessment and Grading

Quality assessment and grading play a crucial role in the harvesting and post-harvest handling of agricultural produce. Accurate assessment of the quality of crops ensures that only the best products are harvested, processed, and delivered to the market. In this section, we will discuss the importance of quality assessment, the factors considered in grading, and the methods used for evaluating the quality of agricultural produce.

Importance of Quality Assessment

Quality assessment is essential for several reasons:

1. Consumer Satisfaction: Consumers expect high-quality products that meet their expectations in

terms of appearance, taste, texture, and nutritional value. Proper quality assessment ensures that only the best products reach the market, leading to increased consumer satisfaction.

2. Marketability: High-quality produce commands a higher price in the market and has a better chance of being sold quickly. Accurate quality assessment helps in categorizing and grading the produce, making it easier for buyers to identify the products that meet their requirements.

3. Shelf Life and Storage: The quality of agricultural produce affects its shelf life and the ability to store it for an extended period. By assessing the quality of crops, farmers and handlers can determine the best practices for storage, packaging, and preservation to maintain the product's freshness and extend its shelf life.

Factors Considered in Grading

Grading is the process of categorising agricultural produce into different classes or categories based on pre-defined parameters. The parameters for grading may vary based on the type of crop, but some common factors considered include:

1. Size: The size of the produce is often an important consideration for grading. For example, in fruits and vegetables, larger sizes may be preferred for certain applications, while smaller sizes may be suitable for processing.

2. Color: Color is a crucial attribute in grading fruits, vegetables, and even grains. Proper color assessment ensures that the produce meets the visual expectations of consumers and indicates ripeness or maturity

3. Shape: The shape of the produce can also be a grading criterion. For example, in potatoes, uniform

and regular shapes are preferred, while irregular shapes may be downgraded.

4. Uniformity: Uniformity in size, shape, colour, and other characteristics ensures consistency within a grading category. This helps buyers in making purchasing decisions and maintaining product quality.

5. Defects: Grading also considers the presence of defects such as blemishes, bruises, insect damage, disease, or mechanical damage. The severity and extent of defects determine the grade assigned to the produce.

Methods for Quality Assessment

Several methods are used for quality assessment and grading of agricultural produce:

1. Visual Inspection: Visual inspection is a common and straightforward method for assessing quality. Trained personnel visually examine the produce, considering factors such as size, color, shape, and the presence of defects. This method is widely used in grading fruits, vegetables, and other visually assessed crops.

2. Instrumental Analysis: Instrumental methods, such as spectrophotometry, refractometry, titration, and sensory analysis, are used for objective quality assessment. These methods measure parameters like sweetness, acidity, firmness, sugar content, and other quality attributes. Instrumental analysis provides accurate and standardized results and is commonly used in grading some fruits, oils, and processed products.

3. Chemical Analysis: Chemical analysis involves laboratory testing to determine the composition,

nutritional content, and presence of contaminants in agricultural products. This method is commonly used for assessing the quality of grains, oils, and processed food items.

4. Microbiological Analysis: In certain cases, microbiological analysis is necessary to assess the quality and safety of agricultural produce. This method involves testing for the presence of harmful bacteria, fungi, or other microorganisms that can cause spoilage or pose health risks.

Chapter Six

Marketing and Selling Peanuts

6.1 Understanding the Peanut Market

The global peanut market has seen significant growth in recent years, with increasing demand for peanuts as a source of protein, healthy fats, and other nutrients. Understanding the peanut market is essential for farmers and sellers of peanuts to make informed decisions about marketing and selling their products. In this section, we will discuss the peanut market, its trends, and the factors that influence it.

Peanut Market and Its Trends

The peanut market is highly dynamic, with several factors that influence supply and demand. Some of the trends observed in the peanut market are:

1. Growing Demand: The demand for peanuts is increasing globally due to their nutritional value and health benefits. The growing demand is driven by factors such as population growth, increasing health awareness, and the popularity of peanut-based products.

2. Diversified Products: The peanut market is diversifying as more manufacturers produce peanut-based products such as butter, oil, snacks, and confectionery. This has increased the demand for peanuts as a raw material, with new opportunities for farmers and sellers as suppliers of high-quality peanuts.

3. Emerging Markets: Emerging markets, such as China, India, and Southeast Asia, are experiencing significant growth in demand for peanuts. These markets present new opportunities and challenges for farmers and sellers in terms of exporting, logistics, and market entry.

4. Supply Constraints: The peanut market faces supply constraints due to factors such as weather, crop diseases, and pests. These constraints lead to spikes in prices and supply shortages, affecting both farmers and buyers.

Factors Influencing the Peanut Market

Several factors influence the peanut market, including:

1. Government Policies: Government policies such as subsidies, tariffs, and trade agreements can affect the demand and supply of peanuts. Policies that

promote exports or impose import restrictions can create market opportunities or barriers for farmers and sellers.

2. Climate and Weather: Climate and weather patterns play a significant role in the production, quality, and price of peanuts. Drought, excessive rainfall, and other weather events can affect crop yields and quality, leading to price fluctuations.

3. Consumer Preferences: Consumer preferences, such as taste, price, packaging, and health considerations, influence the demand for peanuts and peanut-based products. Trends in food preferences, such as vegan and vegetarian diets, also affect the peanut market.

4. Global Competition: The peanut market is highly competitive, with multiple suppliers catering to the global demand. The competition can influence the

prices and quality of peanuts, affecting the profitability of farmers and sellers.

Marketing and Selling Peanuts

Marketing and selling peanuts require understanding the peanut market, consumer preferences, and industry trends. Here are some strategies for marketing and selling peanuts:

1. Focus on Quality: Quality is essential in the peanut market. Farmers and sellers can differentiate their products by offering high-quality peanuts that meet the standards for grading, processing, and packaging.

2. Networking: Networking with buyers, processors, and other stakeholders in the peanut industry can help farmers and sellers identify market opportunities, partnerships, and other resources.

Attending industry events and trade shows can facilitate networking and knowledge sharing.

3. Branding and Packaging: Branding and packaging play a critical role in attracting and retaining customers in the peanut market. Unique branding and attractive packaging can differentiate products and enhance their marketability.

4. Pricing Strategies: Pricing strategies should take into account market trends, competition, and quality considerations. Offering competitive prices while maintaining profitability is crucial for farmers and sellers to remain viable in the market.

6.2 Packaging and Labeling Requirements

Packaging and labelling play a significant role in the marketing and selling of peanuts. Proper packaging ensures product protection, attracts customers, and facilitates distribution, while accurate labelling provides essential information to consumers. In this section, we will discuss the packaging and labelling requirements for marketing and selling peanuts to help farmers and sellers meet industry standards and consumer expectations.

Packaging Requirements

Packaging requirements for peanuts depend on various factors including product type, intended market, and customer preferences. Here are some important considerations when packaging peanuts:

1. Product Protection: Packaging should protect peanuts from physical damage, moisture, pests, and exposure to light to maintain their quality and freshness. This can be achieved through packaging materials such as moisture-resistant bags, airtight containers, or vacuum-sealed packaging.

2. Packaging Size: Determining the appropriate packaging size is important, as it should align with market demands and customer preferences. Consider offering various sizes, ranging from small snack packs to bulk packaging, to cater to different consumer needs.

3. Sustainability: Increasingly, consumers are concerned about the environmental impact of packaging. Using sustainable packaging materials, such as biodegradable or recyclable materials, can appeal to environmentally conscious customers.

4. Branding and Visual Appeal: Packaging should effectively communicate the brand identity and be visually appealing to attract customers. Incorporating the company logo, appealing designs, and eye-catching colours can help differentiate the product and enhance its marketability.

Labeling Requirements

Accurate labelling is crucial for peanuts to comply with regulatory standards and provide consumers with necessary information. Here are some important labelling requirements for marketing and selling peanuts:

1. Product Name: The label should clearly state the name of the product, such as "peanuts" or "roasted peanuts," indicating the specific type or variety if applicable.

2. Ingredient List: An ingredient list should be provided, detailing all the ingredients used in the peanuts. This is especially important for consumers with allergies or specific dietary requirements.

3. Allergen Information: If the peanuts have been processed in facilities where common allergens like milk, soy, or wheat are present, it is important to

include an allergen statement on the label to inform consumers of possible cross-contamination.

4. Net Weight: The label should mention the net weight or quantity of peanuts contained in the package. Providing accurate weight information helps customers make informed purchasing decisions.

5. Country of Origin: Specifying the country of origin on the label is essential for transparency and compliance with import/export regulations.

6. Nutritional Information: Including nutritional information such as calories, fat content, protein, and other relevant nutrients can help consumers make healthy choices and compare products.

7. Shelf Life and Storage Instructions: Labels should include the expected shelf life of the peanuts and any specific storage instructions to ensure the product maintains its quality and freshness.

Compliance with Regulations

Farmers and sellers must ensure that their packaging and labelling meet the relevant regulations and standards in their target markets. These regulations may vary depending on the country and region and may cover aspects such as food safety, labelling requirements, and health claims.

6.3 Identifying Potential Buyers and Distribution Channels

Identifying potential buyers and distribution channels is essential in the marketing and selling of peanuts. With diverse applications in the food industry, peanuts have a vast and growing market. In this section, we will discuss strategies for identifying potential buyers and distribution channels to help farmers and sellers increase their profitability and reach a wider customer base.

Identifying Potential Buyers

Identifying potential buyers is crucial in the peanut market. Farmers and sellers can look for the following types of buyers:

1. Processors: Peanut processors are companies that purchase peanuts for further processing into products such as peanut butter, oil, flour, and snacks. These companies often require large volumes of peanuts and may have specific quality and grading requirements.

2. Manufacturers: Peanut-based food and beverage manufacturers produce products such as candy, confectioneries, energy bars, and milkshakes. These companies may have specific product formulations or grade requirements, and may seek

out specialty peanuts such as organic or non-GMO peanuts.

3. Retailers: Retailers such as supermarkets or specialty food stores purchase peanuts for direct sale to consumers. These buyers may have specific packaging and labelling requirements and may require smaller quantities than processors and manufacturers.

4. Exporters: Exporters purchase peanuts for shipment to overseas markets. Requirements for export may vary by country and can include regulatory compliance, quality assurance, grading standards, packaging, and labelling.

Identifying Distribution Channels

Identifying distribution channels is a crucial step in marketing and selling peanuts. The following are some distribution channels that farmers and sellers can consider:

1. Direct Sales: Direct sales refer to selling peanuts directly to customers via farm stands, farmers' markets, or online stores. Direct sales can help farmers and sellers establish a personal connection with customers and offer fresh and specialty peanuts.

2. Wholesale: Wholesale involves selling large quantities of peanuts directly to buyers such as processors, manufacturers, retailers, and exporters. Wholesale buyers may require specific grades, packaging, and labeling, and may negotiate prices and other terms.

3. Brokers: Brokers connect farmers and sellers with buyers, typically for a commission. Brokers can help farmers and sellers with pricing, marketing, and logistical support, making it an attractive option for those new to the peanut market.

4. Cooperatives: Cooperatives are organizations that bring together farmers and sellers to work collectively to sell their products directly to buyers. Cooperatives can offer benefits such as shared resources, marketing, and distribution networks, which can help farmers and sellers reach larger markets.

Developing a Marketing Strategy

Developing a marketing strategy is crucial in identifying and reaching potential buyers and distribution channels. Below are some steps to consider when developing a marketing strategy for peanuts:

1. Conduct Market Research: Conduct research to determine the demand for peanuts in your target markets, identify the key players, and assess the competition.

2. Determine Pricing: Determine appropriate pricing for your peanuts based on your production costs, market demand, and competition.

3. Create a Brand: Create a brand that differentiates your peanuts from competitors and resonates with potential buyers. Develop branding assets, packaging, and labelling that are visually appealing and highlight the unique features of your peanuts.

4. Establish Relationships: Building relationships with potential buyers and distribution channels is essential in marketing and selling peanuts. Attend industry events, participate in forums and trade shows, and reach out to potential buyers and distributors to establish connections and opportunities to sell your peanuts.

6.4 Building Relationships with Buyers

Building strong and lasting relationships with buyers is critical for the successful marketing and selling of peanuts. By establishing effective partnerships, farmers and sellers can not only secure a consistent market for their peanuts but also gain valuable insights, improve their products, and drive business growth. In this section, we will explore strategies for building relationships with buyers in the peanut industry.

Understanding Buyer Preferences

To build strong relationships with buyers, it is crucial to understand their preferences and needs. Consider the following strategies:

1. Market Research: Conduct market research to gain insights into buyers' preferences, demand patterns, and purchasing behaviours. This information can

help tailor marketing efforts and product offerings to meet their specific requirements.

2. Communicate and Listen: Establish open lines of communication with buyers and actively listen to their feedback and suggestions. Regularly engage with them to understand their evolving needs and expectations.

3. Build Trust: Trust is the foundation of any successful business relationship. Honor commitments, deliver on time, provide consistent product quality, and resolve any issues promptly to establish trust with buyers.

Networking and Industry Events

Participating in networking events and industry gatherings provides valuable opportunities to connect with potential buyers and strengthen existing relationships. Consider these networking strategies:

1. Trade Shows and Conferences: Attend relevant trade shows and conferences within the food industry, such as food processing, snacks and confectionery expos. These events allow you to showcase your peanuts, meet potential buyers, and stay updated on industry trends.

2. Industry Associations: Join industry associations related to peanuts or the food industry. Engage in their activities, attend meetings, and take part in forums to connect with industry professionals and potential buyers.

3. Online Platforms: Utilize online platforms, such as industry-specific forums, social media groups, or online marketplaces, to network and engage with potential buyers. Participate in discussions, share knowledge, and showcase your products to generate interest.

Offering Value-added Services

Providing value-added services can help differentiate your peanuts and strengthen relationships with buyers. Consider the following approaches:

1. Customization: Offer customization options such as flavoured peanuts, roasted to different levels, or packaging tailored to buyers' specific requirements. This can give buyers a sense of exclusivity and cater to their unique needs.

2. Product Innovation: Continuously innovate and improve your peanuts by introducing new flavours, variations, or peanut-based products. Keep buyers informed about these innovations to spark their interest and encourage repeat purchases.

3. Collaboration and Co-marketing: Collaborate with buyers on marketing initiatives, joint promotions, or co-branding opportunities. This can help expand

your reach and create mutually beneficial partnerships.

Providing Excellent Customer Service

Exceptional customer service is vital to building and maintaining strong relationships with buyers. Consider the following strategies:

1. Prompt Communication: Respond to inquiries, orders, and concerns in a timely manner. Keep buyers informed about the status of their orders and proactively address any issues that may arise.

2. Flexibility: Be flexible and accommodating in meeting buyers' unique requirements, such as packaging preferences, order quantities, or delivery

schedules. This demonstrates your commitment to meeting their needs.

3. After-sales Support: Provide post-purchase support, such as addressing any concerns, offering recipe ideas, or providing additional product information. This builds trust and encourages repeat business.

Regular Follow-ups

Consistent and proactive follow-ups are essential for nurturing relationships with buyers. Consider these practices:

1. Regular Check-ins: Stay in touch with buyers on a regular basis to understand their evolving needs and explore potential opportunities for collaboration or new product development.

2. Feedback Collection: Request feedback from buyers regarding product quality, packaging, or any

suggestions for improvement. Actively address their concerns and show a willingness to adapt and improve based on their input.

3. Relationship Maintenance: Invest time in maintaining relationships by celebrating milestones, sending personalized greetings, or acknowledging their support and loyalty. These gestures go a long way in fostering strong connections.

Conclusion

In conclusion, this practical handbook provides a comprehensive guide to peanut farming, covering a range of topics from selecting the right seeds to planting, irrigating, and harvesting peanuts. With this guide's help, farmers can improve their peanut production and increase their yields, leading to better profitability and stronger agricultural businesses.

Furthermore, the guide offers valuable insights into marketing and selling peanuts, highlighting essential considerations such as packaging, labelling, and building relationships with buyers. Farmers and sellers can leverage these strategies to establish strong connections, tailor product offerings to meet customer demands and expand their peanut sales potential.

It is worth noting that high-quality peanut production is essential not only for economic reasons but also for health and environmental reasons. Adopting good agricultural practices, such as proper land preparation, use of pest control measures, and optimal irrigation, can help minimize negative impacts on the environment while producing safe, nutritious, and high-quality peanuts.

Overall, this guide provides a valuable resource for peanut farmers, sellers, and anyone interested in the peanut industry. By utilizing the practical tips and strategies outlined in the guide, farmers can achieve higher levels of productivity, profitability, and sustainability, ultimately contributing to a healthier and more prosperous peanut industry.